The PEOPLE'S PROJECT

ALSO BY SAEED JONES

The PEOPLE'S PROJECT

Poems, Essays, and Art for Looking Forward

CURATED BY
SAEED JONES
AND
MAGGIE SMITH

WASHINGTON
SQUARE PRESS
—
ATRIA

New York • Amsterdam/Antwerp • London
Toronto • Sydney/Melbourne • New Delhi

WASHINGTON SQUARE PRESS

ATRIA

An Imprint of Simon & Schuster, LLC
1230 Avenue of the Americas
New York, NY 10020

First Washington Square Press/Atria Books hardcover edition September 2025

WASHINGTON SQUARE PRESS / ATRIA BOOKS and colophon
are registered trademarks of Simon & Schuster, LLC

Simon & Schuster strongly believes in freedom of expression and stands against
censorship in all its forms. For more information, visit BooksBelong.com.

For information about special discounts for bulk purchases, please
contact Simon & Schuster Special Sales at 1-866-506-1949
or business@simonandschuster.com.

The Simon & Schuster Speakers Bureau can bring authors to
your live event. For more information or to book an event, contact
the Simon & Schuster Speakers Bureau at 1-866-248-3049
or visit our website at www.simonspeakers.com.

Front endpaper credit: Spider Martin/Briscoe Center for American History

Manufactured in the United States of America

1   3   5   7   9   10   8   6   4   2

Library of Congress Control Number: 2025942459

ISBN 978-1-6682-0702-4
ISBN 978-1-6682-0704-8 (ebook)

The ACLU dares to create a more perfect union—beyond one person, party, or side. Its mission is to realize this promise of the United States Constitution for all and expand the reach of its guarantees.

The organization's work spans litigation and advocacy work in all fifty states, DC, and Puerto Rico—including advancing LGBTQ rights, free speech, racial justice, reproductive freedom, criminal justice, immigrants' rights, and others.

The authors and publisher are proud to support the ACLU's tireless work fighting to protect equality and freedom through litigation and public education. We hope you will consider joining the fight to protect civil liberties by visiting aclu.org.

Contents

Introduction

If this book is in your hands, the truth is that you don't need us to explain how it feels to be alive in an era when daggers—seen and unseen, personal and systemic—are being thrown at us from every direction. You know our reality like you know your heartbeat. The fact is that our Present has become the very Past we desperately hoped we had outrun. History, as it turns out, has swifter feet than even the most alert of us could've expected. So then, if you're holding *The People's Project*, what do you need and what, possibly, could the writers and artists in its pages offer?

This anthology is a community as a book. As we put it together, we turned to people who we *always* turn to for guidance, encouragement, and truth. These are the people we text and call to talk our way through the path of daggers. These are the mentors, siblings on the page, and friends we trust with both heavyhearted conversations and laughter loud enough to color a crowded restaurant. We've broken bread, poured drinks, danced, and created art with these folks. And now, as both an offering and a prayer, we're bringing the best of us to you. In a 1982 interview with Kay Bonetti, Toni Cade Bambara said, "As a cultural worker who belongs to an oppressed class, my job is to make revolution irresistible." *The People's Project* is as much about what we need and hope for as it is about who we are.

The fact is, reader, no one is coming to save us but us. Our survival and future—not just through this political era, but onward into the blur of eras that await—wholly depend on our ability to connect with and protect each other far and wide, to share what we've learned from our varied and shared histories in order to enrich one another's wisdom, confidence, and imagination. *The People's Project* is our attempt to honor the fact that, terrified as we are, we are nonetheless proud to understand the stakes of our work. No way forward but through, together. As it should be.

Onward,
Saeed and Maggie

The People's Project

Let's All Stay Alive
by Alexander Chee

The story is an old one: my grandmother in Seoul was said to have buried her sewing machine and silverware in the backyard to keep soldiers from melting them down for bullets. On the surface it has a canny logic, and seems almost wry, even as it speaks to how you might survive the consuming appetite of a war. This was during the Korean War, when my father and his older brother stole food to bring home from overturned army supply trucks—didn't matter whose army—and my grandfather walked the farmers' fields around Seoul for gleanings. If you don't know this word, it is what the farmer leaves behind because it isn't something someone else would buy.

I remember studying the persimmon trees in their backyard many years later, wondering if that was where the sewing machine had been buried. If the silverware I ate from, the frustrating metal chopsticks, the wide soup spoon, if they were those same ones. My grandmother was the kind of woman who would still use them.

Many years later, I read in my grandfather's autobiography the stories he never told us, of a "premonition" that told him and my grandmother it was time to leave Sinuiju, a city along the northernmost border of North Korea and China, where he was working and raising his family, for Seoul. This was the period after the fall of the Japanese Empire and the end of the occupation, before the Korean War began. They left on a business trip with their children, something no one really does, and left behind their sewing machine, family photos, and clothes. What my grandmother buried later would have been the second sewing machine, then, a second set of silverware, perhaps buried because this time she did not want to lose them. The family made a desperate escape conducted in a dangerous boat trip down the western coast, and the boat nearly sank. When I read that, my father's oft-repeated warning, to be a strong swimmer in case the boat went down, came back to me.

I have never been on a boat that sank, but being ready made me ready in other ways, I see now. My father died in 1984 but left me a path I have followed all this way, never quite understanding it until now. If I ever meet him again after death, I will tell him. I am, I was, ready to survive. I did survive.

In my favorite K-dramas there's often a moment when, in the face of annihilating doom, one of the characters says to the others, "Let's all stay alive and celebrate together on the other side." The agreement is to do your best, but also to anticipate joy, to move toward joy. The person who says it does sometimes end up among the dead, but what matters is that it is said, and the group decides to do this. To attempt to survive as an act of love.

It feels like that part of the movie right now. I keep hearing it in my head, so I'll write it here, for all of us: Let's all stay alive and celebrate on the other side. I know it might not be me. But we can try.

Catching the Light
by Joy Harjo

You are a story fed by the generations.

You carry songs, grief, triumph, thankfulness, and joy. Feel their power as they ascend within you. As you walk, run swiftly, even fly, to infinite possibilities.

Let go of that which burdens you. Let go of any acts of unkindness or brutality.

Let go of that which has burdened your family, your community, your nation. Let go of that which has disturbed your soul. Let go one breath into another. Pray thankfulness for this Earth we are—Pray thankfulness for this becoming we are—

For this sunlight touching skin we are—For this cooling by the waters we are—

Listen now as Earth sheds her skin. Listen as the generations move one against the other to make power. We are bringing in a new story. We will be accompanied by ancient and new songs and will celebrate together.

Chile, I'm not playing with you! Look at it!

by Patricia Smith

I.

Chile, I'm not playing with you! Look at it!
My mother, bless her soul, had a habit of grabbing an inch
or so of my nap in her clamped fist, on both sides of my head,
and directing, then holding, my eyes exactly where she wanted
them—an unscrubbed skillet still stinking of ancient oil
and onion, my unmade bed, a gaping front door *letting all*
my damn air out. This time, though, she jerked extra hard
on my Hair-Repped patches, her hands so angry they shuddered.

Don't close your eyes neither! I wanted so much to slam
my sight shut against it, the thing, just this once—scotch-taped
to the door of our Frigidaire, where I'm sure it had always been,
was a picture of a dead boy in his casket. (Black folks, if they
can get away with it, love to snap shots of the departed in repose,
so every few months they can pull the picture down from its
shadow box shelf when company comes and everybody can coo
Lord, he look just like he sleeping. Anything to keep from

saying *dead*.) But our fridge was adorned with not just *any*
dead boy. Ripped reverently from *Jet* in September '55,
four months before my mother screeched my coming,
it was *the* snapshot of Emmett Till, the hot murdered mess
of him spilling over satin, his monstrous head swollen with
regret and Tallahatchie. When I was little, I couldn't stop
looking at him, thinking he was such a stupid reason for a suit.
Look till I say stop looking! my mother bellowed, locking

my hurting head in place, making sure my gaze didn't wander.
And what had I done on that particular Tuesday to merit
such cruel, spectacular punishment? Well, that windy morning
a white man with a pink face had invaded our little apartment,
huger than anything, scrunching his pimpled nose and snorting,
gulping bold glimpses at my mother's trembling chest.
He was there, purportedly, to sell her insurance. I said *yes*
to him once, and muttered *yeah* when he asked me another

question he wouldn't hear the answer to. I did not say *yes sir*
the way I'd been trained and trained to talk to white men,
but not, as my mother called them, *them shifty Negroes.*
The butcher dealing out hog maws in his bloody apron,
the barbers in the corner shop, the nice grocery store man
who hoarded all the best cheap chicken necks for us, none
of them had to be sirs unless you suddenly remembered they
probably should be. No rule was set in place. But white men,

always, girl, always. If you know what's good for you.
Constant in our little roach-riddled tenement, Dead Emmett
was lesson: *This is what white people will do to you if you
don't act right.* My mother gave no indication that the men
who shot and sliced and hammered and strangled and drowned
the boy were totally in the wrong, but if that boy had just
acted right, well—the door of our refrigerator wouldn't look
like that. So the white man came to our apartment that Tuesday

and he stank up the two rooms with his open mouth,
inspected my mother's body like she was balanced on the block,
and I didn't feel that *sir* any kinda way. Now, dammit, I was
going to pay for my disrespect. It wasn't the first time I'd been
forced to *look* at what I had to convince myself was not a boy.
Because through the years, the image of the boy in the casket
stopped meaning *this is what happens to children who don't
act right around white people* and started meaning *this is what*

happens to children who don't act right and that was pretty
convenient for my mother because she could call on Emmett
whenever I hissed underbreath sass to her, when I stayed out
in the streets jumping double Dutch after the streetlights
came on, when I got caught running the faucet and just
pretending to take a bath, when a note came home from school
that read *This child is smart, but she never shuts her mouth,*
when I let that boy look up my dress that one time, and then

that other crazy time when I asked anyone to prove Jesus was real.
My mother's reasoning was *if you don't listen to me about this*
thing you're not listening to me about any thing, and it's just
a matter of time before you make some white person mad
and they kill you. That was my childhood. All my shredded
dreams unreeled underwater. White men wanted to bang on
my body like I was a moonwashed screen door in Mississippi.
Huge gray heads bounced through my daybreaks, and I learned

to live bended so no white person would crave my throat.
I assumed my mother loved me. Meanwhile, the tape sticking
the picture to my whole life yellowed and crackled.
Dead Emmett watched me everywhere. He watched me eat,
watched me watch *Lucy*, watched me kiss the bedroom mirror
I'd named Smokey Robinson. Dead Emmett was a miracle.
Dead Emmett had the nerve to be daddy when daddy was gone.
Dead Emmett ruled the roost. He was hefted like a cross.

II.

There was another picture.
Not the one that graced Emmett with cringing celebrity, not
the one his broken mother Mamie insisted be unleashed upon
a naïve public who had never known that type of twisting,
not the one I never saw peeled from the door of the wheezing
fridge. The other picture was taken in a back room before
the funeral where Mamie presented her son to America and said
This is who the hell you are. The dead boy is there, dead center

on his steel slab, but this time, I swear, there is music playing,
harmonica a sweet slash through the room's flat air. Two other
people are there. His mother, the breathtaking ache, is held tightly
by a man who would later become her husband. The man,
Gene Mobley, glowers at heaven and earth through the lens,
he is a Black man protecting his Black woman, he is wrapped
all the way around her, his fingers press into her arm, his eyes
say *Mamie done had an overload of hurt, now leave her alone.*

While Gene has his word with the world, Mamie gazes at her boy,
taking in the bloated wreckage, the one nostril, the questions where
his eyes once were, the shirt collar threatening to slice into his dead
throat. But in her last moments with Emmett, that's not what she sees.
The music swells to uncanny blue, a sound that rivals love. I imagine
that once the shutter clicked and was gone, Mamie broke loose from
Gene's clutch and rushed to her baby, threw her motherbody against
his strange new weight, and peppered his perfect face with kisses.

Ode to Joy
by Victoria Chang

The wedge of gold near the top, the streaks of
gold dripping down. Frank O'Hara wrote, *No more*

dying. And Joan Mitchell painted a 110½ × 197¼
response. I once believed in the gold because

I was born excessive. Maybe we all are. But how
can I write more like the gold lines near the bottom

of the painting? How can I move radiance forward?
Can language do what a painting does, evoke joy?

Why does language possess some of us, paint
others? A metaphor has a body first, then

a shadow. A chair is a chair before it can be
civilization. A throat as protester, a butcher as

government. In painting, the gold line evokes and
conjures meaning, isn't meaning itself, can skip

meaning. The meaning of words gets in my way.
I have spent my life saying what I mean, but sadly.

Joy must be in separation, in the dripping off after
the sadness. Not for yesterday's sake. I try to

separate language from meaning: *gold minus, gold
wind, gold don't.* No matter how I try, I can't seem

to lose meaning. *Shattered wither, hard-bitten,
disordered else, ruby bloom.* Poor vagus nerve.

Just let the words fall in love. Let me go back to
the beginning of this poem and let it drip down.

My Own Project 2025
by Maggie Smith

A week after the 2024 presidential election, I started a new note on my phone, titled *My Own Project 2025*. I intended for it to be a list of my intentions for the coming year and beyond, a way of articulating—and even revising—how I planned to move through the world.

I texted Saeed: "I started typing up my own Project 2025. First item: no self-abandonment."

What does it mean to abandon oneself? It means to pretend you don't know what you know, don't hear what you hear, don't see what you see. In other words, to gaslight yourself. To stay quiet and compliant. To make nice. To compromise your values to keep the peace, which is not peace at all.

"No self-abandonment" was the first and most essential item, and it leads naturally to the next: We will not abandon one another. We will not disappear ourselves, the way we will not allow others to be disappeared. If any of us is taken, the rest of us will not allow that person to be erased. To be redacted.

We will inscribe ourselves and one another here. That ink is indelible, because it isn't ink at all. Together we are *living* our way into the record. We are writing the story every day, all of us, and we have the power to change it.

Transness as Freedom: An Offering
by Chase Strangio

The first time I found the courage to ask for a haircut that I actually wanted was in 2003. I was twenty-one years old and living in Grinnell, Iowa.

"I look like Hilary Swank playing Brandon Teena in *Boys Don't Cry*." I was laughing, crying, and applying an entire tub of gel to my head when I left the salon with my friend Maggie.

The haircut was terrible and perfect. In my reflection I could see Brandon Teena and somewhere in there I could finally see myself.

Ten years earlier, Brandon had been murdered in Nebraska when he was twenty-one years old.

Later that night my girlfriend broke up with me as soon as she saw me with my new haircut.

Neither the prospect of violence nor of loneliness scared me more than never being myself.

With that haircut, I was liberated from the limiting confines of other people's ideas of what was possible and expected. Even if I was a monster to others, what could be worse than being alien to oneself?

The enduring gift of transness.

It can be unnerving, in a world guided by fear—of change, of the other, as an organizing principle—to let go of others' disgust, rage, and discomfort. But that is what it means to be trans—and what transness offers—an original map unconstrained by another person's limits. No matter how many times and in how many ways my dignity and body have been trespassed upon, since that first haircut, I have been guided by the knowledge of exactly who I am.

Part of what makes trans people so central in this small and toxic moment is the power we wield by being insistently ourselves.

How grotesque, they think, as they try to legislate and punish us back into their boxes. But we cannot be boxed and that is why we hold the map and the key to the future. Trust us when we say leaning into the malleability of binaries and certainties is beautifully expansive.

Transness offers the promise of destabilizing the certainties that built the structures of empire to which our government leaders now cling.

The trans child, the trans worker, the trans elder, the trans ancestor: all have looked other people's certainty dead in the eye and said, "No thank you." If we can do it, so can you. And that is precisely what they are afraid of.

An Education
by Eula Biss

Everyone should have a friend who studies fascism. I met mine, Molly Tambor, in 1999, when she gave me a ride into the city, a three-hour drive. We talked about Emma Goldman—her interpersonal anarchy, her many revolutions—and we talked about the women who were voted into Parliament after the fall of fascism in Italy. Molly hadn't written her book *The Lost Wave* yet. She was doing a PhD in history at Columbia, where she took a course on fascism with Robert Paxton. I was into prose poetry at the time, but fascism struck me as an esoteric interest.

We were at a big band concert sometime in the early aughts when I turned to Molly with the observation that there wasn't a single woman among all the many musicians onstage. The absence of women in a regime, along with low visibility or status for women in the society at large, Molly whispered in the dim light of the theater, is a historical feature of fascism. But fascism takes many forms, and its indicators can shift from one time and place to another. Here is where I started paying attention. Why would anyone need an indicator of fascism?

Years later, in 2017, I returned from a trip to France and read Paxton's *Vichy France* with urgency. A candidate for president who promised to restrict immigration and expel foreigners, who was hostile toward Muslims, an authoritarian candidate who openly appealed to white fears and racist resentments, had just lost the election there, after winning far more of the vote than expected. This was Marine Le Pen, whose supporters shouted "Give us back our house," the house being France. Not long after, an armed crowd would erect a gallows outside the U.S. Capitol before storming the Capitol building shouting "Whose house? Our house!"

I arrived in France from Trump's America while the political graffiti was still fresh on the walls of Paris, where someone had written "Nazi" on a Le Pen poster. The word was a specter from 1940, when half the country was occupied by the Nazis. The Vichy regime, the government of unoccupied France, came into power in 1940 with a project, the National Revolution—a plan to make France great again. This would be accomplished by establishing an authoritarian government, restricting immigration, controlling the press, punishing abortion with the death penalty, persecuting gays, and passing anti-Semitic laws. One of the first acts of Philippe Pétain's government was to repeal a law that banned hate speech in the press. Without any pressure from Germany, his regime went on to revoke the citizenship of thousands of immigrants, a third of them Jewish. This was French fascism. The Nazis, Paxton notes, would have preferred for France to accept the Jews who were being deported from Germany.

In Paris, I stood within the Mémorial des Martyrs de la Déportation and studied a map of France marked with locations of "Camps for Foreigners," among other kinds of detention camps. The history of Vichy France remains a contested history, Molly told me then, exactly because it is so relevant to our time. The United States isn't occupied by Nazi Germans—it's occupied by the same people it has been occupied by since it was colonized. "Occupied territory is occupied territory," James Baldwin writes, "even though it be found in that New World which the Europeans conquered, and it is axiomatic, in occupied territory, that any act of resistance, even though it be executed by a child, be answered at once, and with the full weight of the occupying forces." He is referring here to police brutality, to children beaten by the police in Harlem, and to Black teenagers questioned at gunpoint and sent to prison. The protest of police brutality is, among other things, a statement that we do not want to be governed violently, in an authoritarian manner.

In the fall of 2017, a stadium full of football fans in Boston booed the players who knelt on one knee during the national anthem. The team that was booed was called the Patriots. Among the many meanings of the word "patriot," which is borrowed from the French, is one specific to the United States: "a member of a resistance movement." The New England Patriots are named after this sort of patriot, but that did not settle the debate over whether the Patriots who knelt or the fans who booed them were the "real" patriots.

"Everyone," Paxton writes, "is someone's fascist." The word "fascism" has been so overused, so often understood as a synonym for "bad," that it hardly means anything now, though it has never had one clear definition. Historians have given it dozens of descriptions, stages of development, and lists of defining characteristics. Fascism, Paxton argues, is best recognized by how it works, and it works in a way that is inherently American. "In its adoption of a uniform (white robe and hood), as well as its techniques of intimidation and its conviction that violence was justified in the cause of the group's destiny," he writes, "the first version of the Klan in the defeated American South was a remarkable preview of the way fascist movements were to function in interwar Europe."

Former Confederate soldiers saw themselves as an aggrieved group whose traditional way of life was threatened by freed slaves. The Klan's fascism was dedicated to preserving a social order built around white supremacy. As the historian Carol Anderson argues, "White rage doesn't have to wear sheets, burn crosses, or take to the streets." More often, it works through the courts and the legislature. Where Klansmen used the threat of violence to prevent citizens from exercising their vote, democratic means can also achieve fascist ends. But what it looks like to resist fascism is different in a democracy than it is under an authoritarian regime.

Back in 2016, when I followed the word "resistance" to the French Resistance, I called Molly in dismay after reading a short history of the armed resistance, a history that was essentially a litany of assassinations and executions. There's no place for me, I told her, in a resistance like that. But the armed resistance was very small, Molly informed me. The civil resistance, which consisted mostly of women, was much broader. Women operated safe houses and edited underground newspapers and made forgeries and carried stolen documents in their shopping bags and bicycled hundreds of miles to recover lost radio equipment and pretended not to understand.

The Resistance wasn't singular or centralized. It wasn't a unified left—it was a collection of resistances. There were Communists who organized demonstrations and Catholics who hid Jews and academics who published underground newspapers and railway workers who derailed trains and gangsters who smuggled people out of the country for profit. These resistances didn't share the same mission, or the same motives, but they served the same cause.

There were *résistants*, Molly tells me now, who kept their jobs in the Vichy regime so they could use their positions to falsify papers and help people flee the country. Later, after the liberation, some of them were tried for collaboration. Discerning between a *résistant* and a collaborationist could be difficult, as a person could be both. Some people changed their allegiances, some betrayed their comrades, and some moved back and forth between resistance and collaboration. Resistance was not a fixed position, but a decision that had to be made over and over again.

What would inspire a person to make that decision, the dangerous decision, again and again? Friends, I think. The friends who have been our education, who haven't let us forget about fascism and how it works.

PERFORMANCE SCORES FOR THE ENDINGS AND BEGINNINGS OF WORLDS
by Sam Sax

after Yoko Ono

Score for Formula Shortages

take a brick from the construction
site of a new condominium
      toss it through the window
      of a pharmacy overcharging mothers
record the sound of shattering glass
record the sirens

Score for Private Golf Courses

go at night and plant corn
be prepared to protect your crop
until harvest

Score for the Coming Storms

leave your buckets open to heaven
collect what falls & give it back

Score for a Nonprofit Gala

wear a veil that falls past your feet
haunt the room slow handing out photographs
of every awful thing their money's done—
begin to wail & do not stop wailing
until you or the room empties

Score for Form as a Revelation of Content

every paper you have to fill
out in order to live
feed instead to a fire
   god will speak through it

Score for Landlords

cut a hole in the floor
separate the land
from its prefix, fill the hole
with whatever fruit
would have grown
without you

Score for Organizing Your People

tell everyone you know
to come to what's left
of the town square:
privately owned public park
or target parking lot
assemble in enough numbers
the asphalt becomes
your country

Score for Building Your Own Utopia

there is no where
but here

Raising the Resistance

by Aubrey Hirsch

In the days after the election, I felt all the things.

angry · sad · numb · hopeful · hopeless

And I read all the advice about what I SHOULD be doing.

fight back · seek support · look outward VOLUNTEER · practice self-care · feel your feelings

But I couldn't implement any of it.

I felt frozen.

I felt small.

So I did the only thing there was to do.

I packed lunches.

I worked.

I folded laundry.

I answered emails in the car line.

8 + 6 = 14
9 + 2 = 11
8 - 5 = 3
3 + 7 = 10
12 - 8 = 4
14 - ...
6 - 3 = 3

I checked over math homework.

I was doing what women have always done in the face of fear and fury:

I was getting on with it.

America keeps proving how much it hates women, but it still needs us.

In the months that followed, I've been thinking about what it means to fight back.

And I think the act of resistance I take the most pleasure in is raising my sons to be good men.

I am teaching them to see injustice, to question cruelty, to hunger for a better world.

I get a thrill every time my kids call out misogyny in the world around them.

I'm sure you guys won't be screaming like those girls.

AHHHHHH!

That's kind of sexist.

Or choose kindness.

For: My brother

Or show empathy.

Do you want to play with us?

Standing up to hate is a sign of hope, a belief that we can create a better future.

They can try to take away women's autonomy and our power. But they cannot erase our influence.

It exists in the stories we tell,

in the questions we teach our children to ask.

It lives in dinner table conversations.

in the books we place in eager hands.

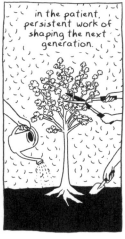

in the patient, persistent work of shaping the next generation.

In the undervalued, unpaid labor of women who are overworked and overlooked.

If they want to force us back into our kitchens,

we will turn them into war rooms.

BATTLE PLAN

If they shove us into corners, we will fight where we stand.

Watching the Valley Oaks
While Waiting to Become Braver
by Ada Limón

I hear the cry of mothers
before the hunting raptor's near.
He rounds circles over crowns
of oaks, and plum, and pear.
Vast beauty, I am frightened—
come beast or hollow air,
the world has been revealed.
Nothing's hopeful, fact, or fair.
But if I fix my senses to you,
in rapt and secular prayer,
and give myself one more hour
to stare and stare and stare,
I might recall my nature too,
and let my little trumpet blare.

Resisting Despair Amidst Know-Your-Place Aggression
by Koritha Mitchell

More than a decade ago, I coined the term *know-your-place aggression* to emphasize that members of marginalized groups are attacked for succeeding, not because they have done something wrong. Their accomplishments inspire aggression as often as praise, but if they don't realize that, they will believe the lie dominant culture tells. Namely, that respect is always granted when earned, so hostility comes only when deserved.

Once someone understands how know-your-place aggression works, however, they notice white mediocrity's truly ubiquitous presence. As everyone obsesses over whether people of color (especially) are worthy, white people ascend while being mediocre or worse. When those considered white have low standards for themselves and one another, they not only give each other success without regard to merit; they also explain away white people's villainy, particularly when those harmed are not white.

Despair can seem the only logical response when one acknowledges this kind of truth. In fact, withstanding despair's allure requires daily self-care practices similar to those that produced my clarity about white mediocrity and white villainy.[1] I value the ability to resist the temptation to believe that my fellow citizens will never be decent toward me and mine. And, if I have found something valuable, I never keep it to myself. My mission is to make every space I enter less hostile for more people and to inspire others to join me in that mission. I take care of myself because I want my life to be a contribution.

For those of us who are constantly under attack, contributing requires prioritizing ourselves *on purpose*. When everything is set up to diminish you and insist that you diminish yourself, defending yourself will only speed your destruction. Our time and energy are better spent on whatever will allow us to embody a proactive stance more often than a defensive posture.

Because Donald Trump became politically relevant by taunting Barack Obama, and brazen indecency has wielded increasing power ever since, I want to explain how understanding know-your-place aggression can align with refusing to give in to despair.

If every victory benefiting someone who isn't a cisgender straight white man will be countered, then the ugliness we're experiencing might be best understood as a measure of our success. Although there are actual casualties and the devastation is undeniable, the backlash should be taken as a reason to continue to build on our achievement. However, especially when we're in pain, we must identify our wins *on purpose,* because our culture's method of retaliation involves turning triumph into a source of shame—via what is most commonly said and done.

As mainstream media has shaped culture over the last decade, it has focused on telling stories that attract engagement by prompting fear, anger, and anxiety. Election 2024 coverage therefore revolved around two narratives: (1) White women betrayed Black and Brown Americans and voted against their own reproductive freedom and (2) Black and Brown Americans betrayed each other.

The latter storyline led to Latino men being newsworthy in ways they rarely are.

If we make a (self-care) practice of considering who is being shamed, we might notice that this (normally ignored) demographic was used to counter a victory. What victory? People were working together to protect a wide range of rights, and they didn't believe the constantly told lie that they needed to downplay their identities in order to do so. From *Win with Black Women* to *White Dudes for Harris*, and from *Muslims* and *Nerds for Harris* to *Hotties* and *Cat Ladies for Harris*, a diverse array of coalitions had worked together to claim full citizenship for groups constantly reminded of their "proper" place of subordination.[2] Nevertheless, the most circulated stories amounted to: women and people of color don't even like each other. These narratives ignore the fact that greater than 40 percent of every demographic, except white men, voted for Kamala Harris. Despite being taught from birth that legitimate authority comes in a white-male package, more than 40 percent of people in most demographics voted for Harris *in order to* protect reproductive freedom, LGBTQ+ rights, and social safety nets and to oppose further destruction in Gaza that would make way for "waterfront property."[3]

Whenever betrayal storylines gained traction, they diminished victories, depicting them as failures so that conditions would remain the same. To view the election's outcome as evidence of marginalized groups betraying each other is to reinforce American culture's low standards for white people, especially white men. Americans don't expect cisgender straight white men to care about others.

However, insisting that marginalized groups betrayed each other also ignores the significant percentage of white male voters who cast their ballot to preserve other people's rights! Specifically, 38 percent of white men cast a Harris-Walz ballot, as did 50 percent of Latino men and 45 percent of white women. Notice how these statistics were reported: as if Black and Brown Americans, LGBTQ+ communities, and other marginalized groups have no allies and no trustworthy alliances.[4]

Precisely because every victory will be countered at every turn, we must make a habit of building on every single success. It therefore matters to notice that greater than 40 percent of most demographics voted for decency rather than for the brazen indecency of Donald Trump and JD Vance. It's also worth noticing that the nonvoter is the biggest voting bloc. As political commentator Clay Cane underscores, only 63.9 percent of eligible voters showed up.[5] A determination to build on victories empowers us to see that people who sat out can become part of the coalition we need.

Notice the difference between the statistical facts and the message sent by what is most commonly said and done. Dominant narratives insist not only that marginalized communities have no allies but also that they deserve none, because they betray themselves and one another. White men holding themselves to low standards is treated as a nonstory because no one truly expects white men to do anything for anyone. Consider how different national conversations would be if major outlets had rigorously examined white men's lack of interest in other people's life chances.

As important, imagine if media coverage had highlighted the 38 percent of white men who voted to make the United States less hostile for more people. Do you remember the traction stories got when based on interviews with the fraction of Black men who loudly found fault with the first Black/South Asian/woman VP? What if prominent outlets had focused on sharing the stories of white men who supported Kamala Harris? Imagine if the resulting narratives had circulated widely.

Mainstream American culture keeps before us that which reinforces the status quo. Rarely seeing examples of white people committed to racial justice encourages folk of color to believe that their fellow Americans will never do better, and it keeps white people who are drawn to justice movements convinced that their inclinations are downright weird. If they seem to be alone in even entertaining it, then solidarity with Black, Indigenous, and people of color must be futile, not worth the attempt. Rarely seeing examples of cisgender and straight people in solidarity with LGBTQ+ communities encourages queer folk to believe their fellow Americans will never do better, and it keeps cis/straight people who are drawn to justice movements convinced that their inclinations are downright weird. If they seem to be alone in even entertaining it, then solidarity with LGBTQ+ communities must be futile, not worth the attempt. Rarely seeing examples of Christians and Jews in solidarity with Muslims . . . (You get my point.) Dominant narratives keep things the same, so we must make a habit of noticing their appeal.

Whatever beats back the sort of progress that makes society less hostile for more people seems to come naturally. However, a self-care practice of identifying know-your-place aggression reminds us that it doesn't. Countering people's capacity to see and value each other actually requires a lot of effort, so it is constantly put forth. Domination does not simply endure; it keeps reacting to every indication that a new day is dawning, every sign that we know we deserve better and are succeeding at securing it. This is why the term *know-your-place aggression* is so clunky; that is what makes it precise. I want us to remain attuned to the constant flow of financial and cultural resources devoted to reversing the success of purportedly inferior people.

If we are to build on victories, we cannot take the bait every time we encounter a story that plays on our fear, anger, and anxiety, especially in a skewed, click-driven media landscape. Our brains love to be proven right, so it may feel good to keep concluding that others will never do better. But it simply doesn't improve what is worth improving: outcomes for ourselves and our neighbors, near and far.

Know-your-place aggression comes in many forms, but the goal is always the same: to send a powerful message about not only how little ordinary individuals think of certain groups but also how little the nation and the world think of them. That's why those who are not cisgender straight white men are attacked—by what is most commonly said and done—*when we are succeeding*. If we make a practice of remembering that, we can support each other amidst the onslaught, recognizing our every victory and deliberately building on each one.

Look Ahead, Look Back
by Jason Bryan Silverstein

The healthcare crises some call failures are, in fact, designs. The knot was not tied by accident. It was pulled tighter with every plantation ledger, every redline, every closed hospital in a town where the coal ran out. Hospitals alone cannot undo what was built to extract, discard, and enrich. To untangle it, we must see it for what it is—a crisis not just of medicine but of history.

The way forward begins with looking back. On the plantation, enslaved people were fed just enough to work. Suffering was converted into capital. The economy had no need for well-being—only for productivity. This plantation logic never vanished. It shapeshifted. Convict leasing in the post–Civil War South operated as a healthcare system inverted.[1] The prison cell became the new slave cabin, where prisoners were kept alive not for their own sakes but for the profitability of their labor.

Bodies remember what power would rather we forget. The Black Belt is now the Stroke Belt.[2] The eighty-five-mile stretch along the Mississippi between Baton Rouge and New Orleans is now Cancer Alley.[3] The racial disparity in infant mortality[4] is higher today than it was during slavery.[5]

Across the nation, maps of segregation predict death with surgical precision. In Boston, life expectancy in the wealthy white neighborhood of Back Bay is ninety-two.[6] Two miles away, in Roxbury, a mostly Black area: sixty-nine. Two miles. Twenty-three stolen years. And so the pattern holds. A ten-year gap between Black and white neighborhoods in Chicago.[7] Eighteen in Columbus.[8] Another eighteen in St. Louis.[9] These racial life expectancy gaps are not because of some biological or genetic difference but because the structures of care were never designed to serve Black people in the first place.[10]

The machinery of neglect grinds wherever power demands labor to feed it. On Navajo land in the Southwest, workers hauled uranium from the earth as radioactive waste crept into their water, all so bombs could be fashioned and the nation could rise. Migrant workers in California—who may have been the last to touch the food many survive on—breathe in chemicals meant to kill insects.[11] When the coal industry collapsed in West Virginia and Kentucky, the jobs and insurance vanished, the hospitals shut down—and in some places came clinics, underregulated and overstuffed with painkillers.[12] Others got nothing at all. In these white mining communities, life expectancy mirrors that in the segregated Black neighborhoods politicians have told them for years to be scared of.

These are not separate tragedies. They are echoes of the same slow violence. The opioid crisis in West Virginia is no different from the one that ravaged Black Baltimore decades before. The poisoned water in Flint mirrors the poisoned wells of the Navajo Nation. These are not failures of the system. They are the system.

What is healthcare if it begins only when the body is broken? Yes, build hospitals—federally funded, community-run—where care was never meant to reach. Expand the National Health Service Corps. Send doctors to the Black Belt, to the reservations, to the neighborhoods where life expectancy has been cut short by design. Wipe away the medical debt that has turned sickness into a sentence. Make healthcare a birthright, free at the point of use, untethered from the cruel arithmetic of who is productive enough to live.

But medicine alone cannot cure what was never just a medical problem. The sickness did not start in the hospital. It started when enslavers devised "calibrated torture"[13] to force enslaved people to meet higher and higher and higher quotas of cotton to satisfy the lust of markets in North America and Europe, from Mississippi to Manhattan to Manchester.[14] It started in neighborhoods built to trap people into "criminal activity," in wages designed for exhaustion, in homes where mold and lead calcify in lungs, in neighborhoods without grocery stores.[15]

The road forward runs through the past. It must reach beyond the exam room into the economy, the environment, the housing courts and zoning boards, the school districts and labor laws, the city budgets and federal prisons. The cure must be as vast as the violence.

Non-Citizen
by Jill Damatac

after Claudia Rankine

You are lit by sunlight, exposed to the outside, magnified by glass. An ant caught on concrete by bored, cruel children on a hot summer day. The café is near where you live, where you hope they won't ever know you live. A friend of a friend, she tells you about her job as a preamble. We the people in this country think work sets you free. She says the guy she's prosecuting is illegal. She says they're all criminals.

You wonder what she sees when she looks at you, petrified while she speaks freely. You tell yourself that Americans talk back, hollow echoes in their self-made chambers. You pause; speaking freely happens only inside your head. You tell her of an undocumented relative, emphasis on this choice of word. You do not say the relative is your mother. Mama taught you long ago to remain silent.

She backtracks; she says she doesn't mean your family, she's sure you're all good people, like she is the judge of this, too. Why does she feel okay saying this to you? You feel shame: this means in plain sight, you have successfully hidden, a traitor in broad daylight. You fantasize about telling the American Bar Association, mutually assured destruction. She will know it was you; it won't matter the cost. Your life is already half lost.

You smile and do nothing, as always. This land is her land, a destiny manifest, her power, blessed, a white heat beaming from a pointed, appointed finger. She is legitimized by elections, votes made by the same people you count on to live. People like you are legitimized by the fruit she buys, the bridges she drives, the care her children live by. None of you are set free by work.

Inside, safe in the cool shaded space of home, you decide: no more new friends. Your true friends are ontological security and emotional capital. That's what the studies say, page after page, about the scars your heart has amassed. Well-being, for you, is any day you get to come back home, safe.

Friends are the ones who stayed despite or because of that one night, when you threw up bourbon, fear, and a secret. The ones who crowd their bodies around bodies like yours, out of unwarranted hands' reach, walking from house to car, car to work, work to work, encircled by arms. Friends who tell them to leave the hospital grounds; this is a place of healing, not harm. Friends who protect children as they sit, like ducks for shooting, in classrooms for learning. The ones who'll rally with poster boards and extra-large markers in DC, patriots of a future country that does not yet exist. The ones who texted you names of pro bono lawyers. Names to save for a raidy day, when men arrive in a parade of pickup trucks and SUVs, one for each year of your life spent hidden, jackboots with trumped-up charges at your door.

A door you will not open because no matter what anyone says, even if it's to your face at breakfast, you still have the right to remain silent. No more new friends; we are each other's friends. The work we do together sets us free.

Noni, Are You Home?
by Aruni Kashyap

after Nilmani Phookan

Noni, are you home? We are expecting rains,
clothes hung on the clothesline, dry rice grains
spread on the cow-dung moped courtyard,
and the goats, the cows, they have returned, looking for
you. Are you home? Why are the doors open?

Noni, are you home? They are saying
four million people are in the holy city
taking dips in the river, washing sins;
are there so many sinners in this
country? How can you just wash away the sins?
Can you wash away blueberry stains,
drop of tea on the white towel?
Noni, are you home? You may have heard

thousands of people ran over thousands.
Others who were sleeping on the riverbank.
Noni, the JCBs are carrying corpses. Noni,
wake up. Are you home? They are hiding the bodies;
relatives are chasing JCBs, visiting morgues; they are
erasing the spots of blood. In the second incident,

many died of thirst. Noni, I saw the young influencer
who was paid to praise the government
lying among the bodies with her mouth open: wide enough
for a rat to go in. Noni, if you fall, it is hard to get up; it is so stuffy
here. Noni, we didn't tell the owner of the shop
that the people lying next to the cold storage
along with the sweets, samosas, milk cartons
were dead. Was it right? Noni, they will
sell those same sweets at high prices to
the celebrities, offer them to the gods.
Noni, there is so much blood.

Here, the price of insulin has risen from six to eighty after
they canceled the Recovery Act; your mother is trying to start
a cooking channel on TikTok after being fired. If you
come down, bring a total of fifteen million dollars, so that
we can buy an American passport: at least we can be
together, Noni. I am tired of living alone, grocery shopping
scares me: what is the news there? Noni:
tell your grandma I do not believe
I will meet her in this lifetime; they are sending
back green card holders at the borders. Tell
your grandma to keep the grains dry,
collect the clothes before the rains arrive.

And. But. Ugh. Yet. Y'all. Mmm. Yes.
by Kiese Laymon

I'm thinking about Jim Henson, the greatest white boy my Mississippi ever created. I'm thinking about *Sesame Street*, the greatest show this nation ever created. The fact that Mississippi created Jim Henson and this nation created *Sesame Street* provides something resembling courage on nights when the United States is abducting college students who protest genocide, killing Black museums, and gleefully sharing war intelligence, with greasy fangers, over Signal.

And.

I don't care if it's money, home training, biscuits, britches, fiction, bullets, bulletproof vests, prayer, clothes, water, swim lessons, poetry, essays, taste, drawers, hoodies, gun lessons, pacifism, tae kwon do, ice cream, headbands, Kermits, rent, or responsible love, I'd like us to share whatever we have in abundance, because Jim Henson and *Sesame Street* taught us to.

But.

Six months after *Sesame Street* debuted, in 1969, an all-white Mississippi State Commission for Educational Television, in the Blackest state in the nation, voted to remove *Sesame Street* from television in our state. Their rationale was leaked to *The New York Times*:

Some of the members of the commission were very much opposed to showing the series because it uses a highly integrated cast of children.

Ugh.

Fifty-six years later, I'm writing this because *Sesame Street* eventually aired in Mississippi twenty-two days later, and Jim Henson kept getting better at art and love. Teachers and parents and regular folk in, and outside of, Mississippi publicly challenged the decision to not air *Sesame Street*. And Black folks in our state never stopped fighting or sharing or believing that the land, and all its possibility, must be shared.

Yet.

Donald Trump is King of the Whites in 2025. And legislators in Mississippi, a place I love more than any other place on earth, the Blackest and poorest state in the nation, decided last month that inclusion, equity, and diversity are now illegal. Unlike sixty-something years ago, Mississippi followed a president who wants to ban PBS and, by proxy, *Sesame Street*, NPR, and Michel Martin. This should break every human heart and collapse all human lungs. The desire to punish those who have already been punished should be breathtaking. In 2025, it is not. It is simply on brand for what the nation has become. We were right about this place.

Y'all.

I remember that in Mississippi, we know how to fight. We know how to lose. We know how to organize with broken hearts. We know how to win. We know how to breathe with collapsed lungs.

My elders used to say that they would never live to see the change they were fighting for. They lied. They saw the change. They made the change. They saw the backlash. Then they died.

Mmm.

I will not live to see the day when Mississippi, *Sesame Street*, PBS, and NPR effectively lead us to a place where all the land is shared and freed. But we will die knowing that our fight for freedom and love of the most vulnerable matters. For that, I am thankful. For that, I am thankful. For that, I am sad as I've ever been.

Mississippi has always been America. Now America must become the best of Mississippi. Yes indeed. Yes.

My Project 2025
by Saeed Jones

after Maggie Smith

I am having more sex.
I am louder when I have sex.
I am asking more questions.
I am asking questions like "Why?"
and "What happened to make you feel
that way?" and "Do you feel safe here?"
and "What can I do to help you feel safe
here?" I know I like to talk; I love the sound
of my own voice, but I'm going to shut up
and listen more. Clearly, I haven't heard
all that's been said. I am protecting myself.
I am pulling up the drawbridge. I'm asking
Black women to pull up the drawbridge.
I'm Whitney Houston in the last verse
of "It's Not Right but It's Okay." I'm
paying my light bill and taking care
of my babies. I'm in the bathtub
covered in bubbles and surrounded
by candles and good wine and I wish
Frank Ocean or Bill Withers or Frank Ocean
and Bill Withers were in the bathtub

with me, but their voices will do. I am
pulling the voices of people I desire
and love and trust and worry over
into me. I am inviting them into the bright
dark of my soul. I am gonna live forever,
because all the money I touch looks at me
and says "e pluribus unum"—out of many,
one. I am the water Jesus drank in the desert.
I am god talking to herself. I am evicting
America from my body and making room
in the borders of my Black bad bitch body
for everyone I was sent into this life
to love loudly.

Snail's Pace: The Art of Cripping Time
by Alice Wong

What we do with our time and the expectations of being productive under the weight of rapid response and long-term organizing is profoundly ableist. Urgency is often conflated with speed. Yet the fear, chaos, and danger many of us live in change our relationship with time. To fight, to provide mutual aid, to listen, care for, and love our people, to nourish and sustain yourself—all of these things take time and energy. We must give ourselves space, grace, and time if we are to fight fascism. The work will always remain, waiting for us. To have the discipline to slow down is an exercise in restraint when your body is screaming to fight or flight amidst a wildfire fueled by hate. In these times (and all times) look to your sick and disabled comrades.

We know how to live with uncertainty, unruly bodyminds, and constraints beyond our control. Disabled people have such survival skills that come from living in a world that actively seeks to erase us. To crip something is to imbue it with disabled wisdom. Crip time is revolutionary and liberatory. To live in crip time requires us to dismantle the ableism that tells us our value is tied to our productivity. Crip time rejects linear, monolithic ways of thinking of being. In an essay by Dr. Ellen Samuels, crip time "requires us to break in our bodies and minds to new rhythms . . . It forces us to take breaks, even when we don't want to, even when we want to keep going, to move ahead. It insists that we listen to our bodyminds *so* closely, *so* attentively, in a culture that tells us to divide the two and push the body away from us while also pushing it beyond its limits."[1] Most, not all, of my activism is with other disabled people and the difference is palpable. There's an implicit understanding that we run at different speeds and modes, that there is no shame in not keeping up, dropping out of a project, or canceling a meeting. Slowing down. Resting. Listening. These are acts against the tyranny of the clock and everything considered normal, valuable, and good. They allow us to fight the powers that be and love ourselves and one another at the same time.

In the first year of the pandemic I was lonely and felt an empty hunger. A friend found a snail in his produce and remembered my fondness for them. A few frantic online searches later I got a terrarium and learned about feeding it. Augustus the snail was a delight. His shell was a brown decorative swirl, and his body, which acted as a foot, glided up and down the branches I placed in his little home. I spritzed water in the glass cube every day to provide a humid environment and enriched the soil with bugs. Once in a while I dropped a piece of napa cabbage and watched him slowly move across the entire leaf, landing on the sweetest, curly green part of the leaf. Augustus munched and munched and munched some more. His little munches filled me up. There would be times he hid for an entire day under a piece of bark, not moving a millimeter. In his stillness Augustus taught me the art of cripping time. He didn't care about my schedule. Augustus existed in his own dimension and gave me the joy of caring for another living creature. I learned to wait and not expect anything. His pace was his own, as was mine.

For Hope
by Abi Maxwell

In the summer of 2020, my family moved to a new home. On the second day there, we found focaccia wrapped in wax paper on the back step. I told my daughter that a neighbor must have dropped it off, which was lucky, because we didn't have groceries yet. We sat down to eat. But then I stopped us. What if the meal belonged to someone else? What if it was rotten? What if, impossibly, it had been poisoned?

I hadn't always been like this. One year earlier, the small New Hampshire town where my ancestors had lived for centuries had risen up against the rights and existence of our daughter through a series of monthly school board meetings and, in time, a parent group built to target her. She was six, then seven. My husband and I became human shields, and eventually—because of a state nondiscrimination law signed just that year—we were able to get a school policy passed to protect her legal rights. But the damage was already done. What future could our daughter possibly have in a place where classmates told her she wasn't allowed to be a girl? Where even the superintendent made a rule that the word "transgender" could not be used in the classroom setting?

The country was in Covid lockdown when we sold our house and left that town, and all three of us—my husband, our daughter, me—were awash in constant vigilance. Everything, everyone, had become a threat to our lives. But also, what had become of our will to live? We had been stripped down, turned inside out, harmed not by strangers but by people who'd spent generations eating the soup my grandfather had made for his church.

My husband and I had wanted to leave the state, to get as far from that place as we possibly could, but the pandemic meant we couldn't find new jobs. Besides, in New Hampshire our daughter at least had legal protections, which was not the case in most states across the country. So we found a house on the outskirts of a small city just thirty miles from our old town, and after that focaccia arrived on our back step, more gifts just kept appearing. Fresh eggs, cakes, homemade ginger beer. Sheep's wool to hang from the trees as a gift for the birds to build their nests. Books of folklore. Once, newly hatched chicks, tucked into a McDonald's Happy Meal box.

By the time those baby chicks arrived, I knew Hope. She lived up the hill from us, on the far side of the field, and she'd started to call or stop by multiple times a day. She'd tell me to watch my cat because the hawks were circling above. That she had too much ice cream in her freezer and wanted to give me some. That she was wondering if she had ever told me the story about the time she let the owner of the pet shop talk her into bringing a monkey home for the kids.

"That was a fucking mistake," she said. She loved to swear. "Abi!" she once shouted at me, the moment I answered the phone. Her classical music was blasting in the background—it always was. "I've lost my fucking bees! Have you seen a swarm in your yard?"

Hope was in her eighties by that point. When she was younger, she'd been a photographer who specialized in a technique from the 1800s called gum printing, and although she had a darkroom, she'd preferred to develop her work in the sunshine, where the results became more varied and mysterious. By the time I knew her, her fingers had turned so thick with arthritis that she couldn't develop her photos anymore; yet in the early days of the disease, she'd heard that bee venom could relieve the pain and swelling, so she learned beekeeping and then caught two bees a day and had a friend hold them to her hands for a sting.

Eventually, Hope and I would walk the field between our houses together every afternoon. Sometimes as we walked, I'd tell her that I feared my family would have to move again. That instead of fighting a town, I was suddenly fighting a state, because New Hampshire legislators had started to introduce bills to block our daughter's rights—even her right to healthcare. That the worst of the legislation would not only ban the medicine that afforded our daughter a happy, healthy life—or, truly, any life at all—but also remove her from our home and convict her father and me of child abuse.

Every time I told this to Hope, it was like a fresh shock to her system. She'd abruptly stop walking, so I'd stop, too. She'd grab me by the upper arms. Her eyes were deeply set by that point in her life, tucked behind folds of skin, and I remember the way they would move quickly, back and forth, as she stared at me. It was like she was digging, searching around for some piece of me to catch.

And then, "Would you look at those clouds," she'd say. She'd point to the Japanese knotweed strangling the trees out and say, "Isn't it so beautiful, the way the light hits?" Once, it was a snowy egret, a bird we had never seen in that area before. We'd just crossed the lowest section of the field and were headed back up. Fog hung so heavily that we could scarcely make out the shape of the field's lone tree in the distance. I was terrified; I was always terrified, because there was always more legislation to fight. Hope stopped, grabbed my arm. Our dogs stopped, too. The bird— glowing white through the fog, tall and all alone—just stood there before us. Hope dug her camera out from her coat pocket, a small digital thing that she brought to the developer in town weekly. The bird—an apparition that even the dogs could sense—just kept standing there, holding us steady. And then it flew away, and we walked on.

Hope died just four years after we moved to that hill, and in the same season my worst fears for my home state came true— legislation to remove my daughter from the state's nondiscrimination law passed through the house and senate; she was banned from playing sports with other girls; the first official step in banning her medical care was signed into law. I spent a few weeks focused on the pain of my heart splitting in half. One day, I collapsed in the shower. But then I peeled myself up and grabbed the first chance I could find to move my family to a place where our daughter could be whole; within days of the legislative news, we were once again packing our house, this time to move across the country to California.

In the final months of her life, Hope passed many of her gum prints on to me, and now her ethereal sweeps of cyans, magentas, and yellows hang on almost every wall in this strange new space three thousand miles from our previous home. One of her favorites hangs in my kitchen. It's the shadow of her husband—who died long before I met her—arms held high above his head. When she'd developed the photo, a glowing sphere of light had appeared. In the print Hope kept, the sphere landed right between her husband's hands, making it seem that he was holding up all the light of the world. In my copy, the sphere is slightly off-center, just barely within reach, which now feels like a very purposeful gift from her to me. I look at that print, at that miraculous burst of light, and I will it to ferry me back from terror to my kitchen—to the coffee in my hand, to the call of the crow in the redwood outside my window. Sometimes, I walk through the apartment that I still have not learned to call my home and I look at all of Hope's photos, one after another after another. On the hardest days, I even run my hand right over their rough surface, just grasping for the proof I know they can give me—that we can manifest the light that is already there.

Good Pain!
by Tiana Clark

ending with an epigraph by Zadie Smith

Sometimes the wound is sacred.
The damage makes us more whole.
Sometimes crying is the commitment
to more joy. I've learned survival, like grief,
is not linear. A circle has no starting place,
each place is a chance to love the moment
you are in. Each place is a moment
to see the winter jasmine blooming
bright yellow buds during the bleak
morning walk around the periphery
of the lake, making sure not to step
in the Tetris of geese shit, which makes
me think of Mary Oliver's poem,
especially the honking sound of the geese,
which is not altogether beautiful,
but a wild call waking me up to a world
of my unfelt feelings. Oh, my feelings!
Like Glück, I have so many of them too.
I used to be afraid to fully feel the violent rush
of them throttle through me in all their gorgeous

power before the divorce, before the panic
and stress from first-book energy. Before
I knew how to breathe properly. Before
I knew how to sit still and melt. Before
I was diminished by my desires until I learned
how to name each one with audacity. Before
when I carried the awkward weight
of my sadness like some fucking trophy.
Long-suffering is not a virtue. I'm done
with martyrdom. Suffering is not my name.
I claim joy as my birthright by casting
the cross off my back. Death is not meant
to be carried but surrendered. It's about trust,
and yet, young students keep asking me questions
about success. I answer, *What's the rush?*
But I remember asking the same questions too.
We valorize early achievement and then what?
We are all so busy with wanting to become
that we forget the becoming. I remember
David Baker saying, *There is no hurry.*
I finally understand that now. Though
that understanding happened with distance
and privilege. Still the emphasis is on the process
not the product. The poem starts brewing
long before the words slice the page
and when the tornado ripped a scar
through Nashville in March 2020,

I was sitting in my bathtub at 1:07 a.m.
with my dog in my lap, covered with pillows,
calling my soon-to-be-ex-husband, who did
not answer. Later my therapist said, *No one
is coming to save you.* Ouch, Brenda, that hurt . . .
really good! I realized then that I was the one
I had been waiting for. I realized I could protect
myself from anything that would try to destroy me
and abundance—yes, abundance—was the blood-
rusted Japanese maple I saw on another walk
around the same lake during the pandemic
when all I did was walk, move my body
forward and more forward when I felt stuck.
The tree was already magnificent inside me.
The natural world mirrors back your music
and metronome. I was done with the lack.
The validation inside my chest, reverberating.
I crave resonance now. The uncertainty
is the only certainty we have, which means
I have to keep trusting that who I am right now
is enough. Whatever I am working on right now
is enough. I know you have so many questions.
I do too. Sometimes I know how to answer them.
Other times I am still living them by living through
them à la Rilke, right? I am still improvising,
making it up like Clifton, conjuring bridges across
the chasms, holding my one good hand like my mother

did when she gave birth to me. I am still asking better questions of my questions. Let's take a deep breath:

We were heading toward all that makes life intolerable, feeling the only thing that makes it worthwhile. That was joy.

Fix Up, Look Sharp
by Marlon James

So, I have been dressing a lot more extra since November 2024. More expensive, more layered, more Yamamoto. Some people, knowing my knack for dandiness, might find that first sentence redundant; after all, I am the fashion victim who has a crisis before heading to the gym. My home gym. I'm also that forlorn vampire roaming the streets of New York City at night because the party ended early and I'm dressed too damn good to just go home. But better clothes have been finding me lately, and I think I know why. Back in 2015 on a writers' panel in London I said that before the Black woman joins the struggle she must first make sure her clothes are on point and her hair is well did. A white feminist news commentator attempting some version of clapback said that my idea of feminism was one step forward, two steps back. This was sad, and not because of the use of cliché, but because homegirl thought she was some enwokened Black ally yet had no clue about the long tradition of resistance and rebellion via Black glamour. To misunderstand that was to misunderstand Blackness itself. Massa was always perplexed by slave self-presentation because one of the goals of slavery was the obliteration of self. And after four centuries of slaveryjimcrowseparatebutequalredlinebluelivesmattertrump, Black dress-up remains our most vital route to self-possession. Religion likes to claim that position, but for that to work you'd have to let someone else possess you. There's a reason why rappers name-check fashion brands, a reason that mystifies even the Black intellectual class. Because if you have had even a little something, then you might not understand the drive to possess anything. It's not enough that I make a stand when the oppressors come. It's important that I'm wearing my best suit or maybe a long black dress. So yeah, Black self-possession. Nowadays I find that the only way I can move in this world is to leave home presenting my very best self. I dug out my bell-bottoms because I knew they'd come back. I wear all black because all black slims the shit out of me. I wear platform boots because the seventies was the best decade and I like looking the best me. I also wear boots because any day now I might need to stomp the shit out of a Nazi or run for my life. I wear clothes so that people will think twice before sitting beside me on the bus. My belt buckle says, DON'T START NOTHING AND THERE WILL BE NOTHING. My tux jacket and kilt tell 2025 that I'm both coming from and going to somewhere better. I will take society's tripe and make chitlins, put some back into Balenciaga, bulge the hell out of my vegan leather pants, squat in spandex at Equinox gym, and scribble on a pair of Yeezys that Kanye should take his fucking meds. I'll burn my skinny suits because that is now what fascists wear. I will look in the mirror and tell it to tell the seven wonders to wonder. These days I'm not just putting on clothes, I'm putting on armor. I want something that smells an awful lot like victory. So I look to Toni Morrison, Toni Cade Bambara, and Ntozake Shange—their wardrobes this time, not just their books—and head out looking like I've already won this war.

Feb. 2024

The Right Question
by Ashley C. Ford

I don't love giving advice. I don't like telling people what to do. I don't often think of myself as a person who gives advice, because I don't often think of myself as someone with enough experience, expertise, or authority to be giving advice.

I know there are some basic things we should get when we're young (love, guidance, affection, etc.), and very basic things we should be able to get from one another (compassion, respect, the benefit of the doubt, etc.), but beyond that, I suspect I'd have to consistently be around a person for a month minimum before I could suggest anything useful to them about their own life.

If I'm honest, I'm not sure what my standards are for someone who would be worthy of offering advice to others, little parables, and thought exercises you'd actually expect to improve the lives of the people around you. I know what has worked, and what continues to work, for me, but I don't pretend to have any answers about what should work for everyone else.

That might all be bullshit, though.

The truth is, I tend to undersell and underestimate myself *to myself* most of all. It could be that I would be exceptional at getting people to look and reflect upon their own lives, and find within that reflection the answers they seek from me. But even if I don't know how to tell people anything about anything, maybe I do know how to ask them the right questions. That feels right to me.

Among the most useful skills I've developed, seemingly by accident, has been asking myself the right questions at the right times. I remember asking myself in the seventh grade how much of my true self I was willing to sacrifice to fit in better among my peers. Before college, I questioned whether or not I could live in a new place while belonging to a family I knew wouldn't come to me. I spent the two weeks before I moved to Brooklyn from Indiana arguing with myself about whether it was courageous or foolish to move to New York City, alone and on crutches, with a busted ACL.

Sometimes, I resist asking myself the questions I most want answers to because I already know I won't like the answers, and once I know the truth, I won't be able to lie to myself about it. Then everything will have to change. As a rule, I am resistant to change. The truth of this makes me afraid that the preternatural fear that seemed to gobble up the common sense and casual affection of my family members is genetic. I worry I'll always be hesitating, resisting, and waiting too long for someone else's approval.

Despite this worry, I've been making room for all of me in the world, even in the spaces that are purposefully narrow. If I want in, I find my way in. If I want to know, I find out. And if the road doesn't seem worth the destination, I'll honor myself enough to find a different path toward something better for me. My desire does not always have a destination. Sometimes it's just an arrow pointing in the general direction of whatever comes next.

None of the "advice" I offer other people is meant to be a destination. The question asked is meant to be a gentle nudge, another arrow piercing the air toward their own desires, their own curiosities, and a life experience more consistent with where they feel they belong. I don't want to tell anybody what to do. I just want to ask a few questions, and I want us all to figure out our own answers in our own time. That feels right to me too.

Portrait of Myself as a Boat
by Kay Jones

When I was very pregnant, I thought of myself as a boat. Not in the sense of "big as" but as a vessel charged with ferrying a small purple creature with an implausibly big head and square fists to shore. I was ferrying and building from the inside out, never in doubt of what my body "ought" to be doing or look like, unlike how I had often felt in my unpregnant body. My boat-self sliced through the water at the swimming pool, my abdomen a bow navigating the cereal aisle.

In 2016, my due date approached and a person I absolutely did not want to have any kind of authority over me and the people I loved was elected. I'd wanted a kinder and gentler world to usher my small passenger into, so the longer that kid wanted to stay in there the better, as far as I was concerned, even as the sides of the boat strained and the child made their impatience with the constraints on their movement known. Eventually the purple child with the square fists had to be ushered out, into the world, and the doctors pronounced the child a healthy _____.

We'd known of course that the child had or did not have certain chromosomes from early on. We had used the idea presented by those chromosomes to whittle down our list of names. The name we chose was beautiful and strong and went with the chromosomes we thought we knew how to read.

But as an editor and reader, over a lifetime I've learned that so much of what we know and understand is based on interpretation, a process that is inexact and highly subjective and that may shift over time owing to a number of factors.

The child grew and we delighted. We fed and loved and read our child stories, and danced and sang, dressed them in clothes they loved—stripes and bright colors, shirts with diggers, hot pink shorts with flowers on them. A skirt to twirl in. Socks I bought specially because they were the only ones that stayed on.

When the child began to speak, they spoke with certainty and authority. "I am a _____," letting us know we'd read things wrong, all of us—the doctors, the tests, the machines.

Well, we thought, how can we be sure?

What does gender mean to a child, I asked myself. Was this the reaction of a new consciousness perceiving the dynamics of regimes of power that do not favor women? The aftermath of childbirth had taught me that our country does not provide adequate postpartum support for people, that just having had a baby accorded me little to no accommodation in spite of the tremendous resources I was now expending in the service of taking care of said baby, much less myself. Had I, a woman, somehow demonstrated my lack of power, my lack of value to my small person?

An analysis of gendered power dynamics is a lot to credit a small, barely verbal person with, I know. But I wondered back then. And I worried.

In retrospect I know it's better to ask what any of us knows, with any kind of certainty, about reading chromosomes.

Time passed. I have been fortunate to have flexible work and a supportive partner. I delighted in my child, and made sure to clear time to talk with the kiddo every day, just talk, about nothing and everything. I marveled then and now at how my child never wavers in their sense of themself—never wavers in the way I have at times wavered about my own gendered sense of self.

One spring when my child is three or four we go to the doctor's office and have to fill out a form. For the first time, somehow, they have their choice of pronouns and the ability to understand what a pronoun stands in for. The delight with which he chooses his pronouns and watches me ink the dot on the form is unequivocal.

Soon after, he asks us to use he/him pronouns—only at home, for now. Later, he and I travel, and he asks to be introduced to new people as my kid, as opposed to son or daughter, for now. He is very clear in his wishes. His sense of self is not a mistake, not a confusion.

All this while I am on a mission to read everything I can find for parents of small, gender-expansive children, which is not much. I talk with experts in early child development, with friends, doctors, teachers. I learn the terms "gender nonconforming" and "gender expansive," and I search the web for information about how soon a child can develop a sense of gender.

The threads of wonderment and admiration and joy and pride but also ones of worry and what-if are weaving together in my consciousness. The what-ifs grow, and with them the worry. What I am seeing on the news happening to trans people is devastating. How will I protect my child? How will I keep him safe?

One day, I'm on the phone with a poet friend who asks about my child. And I decide to be honest. I say, Well, the kiddo is doing great, thriving, and says that we got the chromosomes wrong. [*pregnant pause*] And I'm scared.

The poet takes a beat and says, with real delight and emotion in his voice, "I'm *excited* for y'all!"

I take a breath. I exhale and feel so much washing off of me, like when you wipe a dirty window clean. I know the poet is right. I feel a little ashamed, because in all my fear, what I've missed is the flip side. The flip side is this: I as a parent have the opportunity to focus on what is right rather than what is wrong. I know, as sure as I know that my hand is attached to my wrist, that I will support, and care for, and advocate for my child as best I can until my dying day and hopefully beyond. I will navigate this as I would navigate anything else for my child. I choose my child, and I choose the joy of supporting my child and other families yet to come.

I am a boat again, a different kind of boat, I think. An icebreaker.

One spring the kid is on a tire swing with a bunch of other kids, and much is being made of the fact that it's an all-girl tire swing, and the kid yells at the top of his voice, "I'M NOT A GIRL, I'M A BOY!" and the parent pushing the swing says, "Okay, it's *not* all girls on the swing!" and looks at me and raises his eyebrows. And then the other parents standing around look at me and raise their eyebrows too. I smile and nod. I say, "He's a boy, and he uses he/him pronouns." The parents all nod and smile back and say, "Okay! He/him!"

Later, I answer their questions, and they answer those of their children, who are mostly much better at understanding than adults are. We tell the doctors, and the teachers, and a year or two later the kid sheds the name that is wrong and takes one that is right, and with joy I quickly attempt to edit everything that has his name on it. Some systems prove more difficult to edit than others, but we persist.

Harder conversations have come and will yet come along. There has been some loss and grief, a letting go of people I never thought I'd need to let go of but who do not or will not understand that my child's sense of self is not up for debate. Luckily, family is also not derived only from shared chromosomes.

For me, underpinning everything now is the joy of the possibility the poet pointed toward. My partner and I have a chance to get things right for our son, who has shared with us a fundamental truth about himself. How lucky we are to be able to protect him by accepting him. How lucky we are to live in a state where that is possible. How lucky we are to have a kid who tells us who he is.

Return Ghazal
by Hala Alyan

The house smells of what you last burnt: rice, cedar, wick.
In forty-eight or twenty-four, there's a lifetime between return,

a criminal dream. How many child braids does it take to build
a moon? How many du'as of a green return?

I'm sorry. I'm late. The only antidote for the looking is more
looking. The ancestors are restless. They dreamed return

and got bodega junipers instead, fairy lights on a fire escape, daughters'
daughters thrifting Polaroids and silk. Did they mean return?

My parents arrived so I could become a shrine. Here's salt
to break a curse. Here's an American mouth saying no. Here's return,

tugged forward like a boat, cutting through blue water.
My inheritance: English suras, pearl rings, lemon trees, Salim's return.

I don't want your country or your concession. Say genocide. Say again.
Butcher, bomber, hot mic. The earth heard and the earth teemed, returned

to the birds, returned to itself. I've tasted Haifa's sea.
I've walked to the edge of the earth. I've seen return.

Time of War
by Danez Smith

      i.

the first thing you need to understand is fear:
its nine arms, its three mouths, its million eyes all shut

the first thing you need to understand is fear
is a monster with its eyes closed
not out of fear, but fear of guilt
so it's the soul, the soul's eyes closed as coins

the first thing you need to understand is fear
is a monster the size of a mushroom cloud
its soul's eyes closed its dance a cruel gravity
reckless and flattening and the blood staining its feet

the first thing you need to understand is fear
is a monster throwing a tantrum in a city
eyes closed tears leaking
the people below drown as it weeps
and it weeps drones and smoke and snipers
it weeps bombs and phosphorus and weeps the bread away
it weeps rape and prisons and propaganda
it weeps blue flags and blue dollars and blueprints

to build where they blew us up
the things the things the people drown in
would make fear cry if fear opened its eyes to see them

the first thing you need to understand is fear
is the size of a bomb is the soul's eyes closed
is the history used as context to kill the future
is the future has a price is the future is lonely
for her dead sisters is the future is free so it's scary
is fear hates freedom throws bombs
with its eyes closed into what it sees as darkness
with its eyes closed it throws bombs at nothing
with its eyes closed your life means nothing to fear
as your life burns and chokes on the dust of being
made nothing fear is the size of nothing
we've ever seen so big it starts to look
not like fear but like greed it looks like it's crying
it's eating really eyes closed mouths open
those aren't tears it's spit how did we get in its mouth?

the second thing you need to understand is money:

    ii.

the question reaches its dust-blinded, water-starved hand
scratching in the seven directions of time—

                        where is my child?

meanwhile, in America, someone changes the channel to cartoons
in America, we don't need our enemies' help to kill our children.

iii.

i worry who i would be
if you handed me
a map
and a gun
and told me
i could be free.

iv.

Ms. Jordan, i know. i know. thank you for passing the knowing:
My captor's brother is my captor, too.
My captor's brother's captee the other half of my key.
The key, if not in reason, in the captor's felled heart.

v.

get it right
                Martyr
doesn't mean they killed me
                Martyr
means the victory will be made of my name.

vi.

the moon is full
which means
again we are in the light of god
and again
the light will turn from us

again into the darkness
trying to find a witness
or a savior
and found only
myself

so left to chaos
i become the rain
and find my center
reroute the storm
to my will.

You Are Here
by Mira Jacob

Leaving this here so you have it to come back to today. This country has always been brutal, and there has always been an us who have been fighting it. The beauty that comes out of that fight, the way our love for each other changes the world around us, is real and glorious and unrelenting. It cannot be caged, tamed, erased, or lost. You are part of that tradition. I know you are starting to know this, but really *know* it now. Art is making something no one asked for—not because they didn't need it, but because they didn't know they needed it until you made it, until it helped them breathe and dream and find a way forward. It's part of a map that shows us how we get out of this place. Keep going. Do your part. Love you—Mom

Weathered Hands
by Imani Perry

My ancestral tree is a bald cypress. Some branches are chopped, but the roots stay spreading (knobby knees break sidewalks open) and the leaves still come in spring.

The people who raised me lived in a world of colored signs, beans instead of meat six days a week, dogs trained to terrorize Black folks, bombs planted to shatter us, underfunding, overtaxing, and hunger pains for freedom offered in supplication on Sundays, in schools, in fields, in cells.

That old cypress tree was hardy. I was raised to look in the mirror and see promise and beauty. My aunties would tease us, the grandchildren, saying, "Y'all are so vain," as we gazed at ourselves, elbowing each other, not a one doubting that our faces mattered. My aunties' words were not admonition, but sincere amusement mixed with love. I marvel now, at how they gave us such unabashed admiration for ourselves, Black children of the red clay, of the land that slavery made.

That inheritance is now a duty to pass down.

Today I ask: How do we raise the young in the face of deportations, expulsions, captivity, abandonment, and targeted cruelty? How do we feed those writhing with hunger pangs for freedom? Feeling the chopped branches, how hard for them to hold fast to the trunk—how to convince them not to fall? I must admit, I feel less competent than the people who came before and so I beg merciful inspiration from those ancestors as I look into the tear-filled eyes of the young, queer, Black, Brown, disabled, poor, imprisoned, captive, neglected, abandoned.

Teach me. Teach us how.

Hugging the cypress, I say a prayer:

If I/we achieve nothing else in life, won't we please care enough to give the best of what we've received to the ones coming behind us so that they might create where we have failed. Won't we teach them to love beyond our backyards, past our borders of nation-states, faith, tax brackets, and identities. Won't we hold up an honest mirror to the beauty of those marked least and shoulder their inheritances (our duty) forward, which itself is a promise: "my weathered hands, my aching heart, they are yours."

Puzzle
by Randall Mann

Something ends. Something else begins
in a knowable shadow
like a partner.

Honestly, I prefer silence.
A pollster spins: words matter—
what we say, fail to say—

more than enunciation.
The point is,
maybe nothing is pointless.

I have seen, in this puzzling time,
few acts of compassion.
If truth is lazy, like poetry,

let me state this clearly:
I've been numbed by what I have seen
in the distance, signs

in the distance, signs
I've been numbed by. What have I seen?
Let me state this: clearly,

if truth is lazy like poetry,
few act. Of compassion
I have seen, in this puzzling time,

maybe nothing is. Pointless?
The point is
more than renunciation.

What we say fails to say.
A pollster spins words, matter—
I prefer honesty. Silence

like a partner,
an unknowable shadow . . .
Something ends. Something else: begin.

Notes

Resisting Despair Amidst Know-Your-Place Aggression *by Koritha Mitchell*

1. Koritha Mitchell, "Identifying White Mediocrity and Know-Your-Place Aggression: A Form of Self-Care," *African American Review* 51, no. 4 (2018): 253–62. See also Harvey Young, "White Mediocrity Empowers White Villainy: A Conversation with Koritha Mitchell," *Public Books*, May 15, 2024, https://www.publicbooks.org/white-mediocrity-empowers-white-villainy-a-conversation-with-koritha-mitchell, and Koritha Mitchell, "I'm a Black Woman Who's Met All the Standards for Promotion. I'm Not Waiting to Reward Myself," *Time*, April 27, 2021, https://time.com/5958844/black-woman-self-care.

2. Koritha Mitchell, "Identity Groups Are Mobilizing for Kamala Harris. That Shows Progress," *Time*, July 29, 2024, https://time.com/7005092/kamala-harris-identity-groups-zoom-calls.

3. Patrick Wintour, "Jared Kushner Says Gaza's 'Waterfront Property Could Be Very Valuable,'" *The Guardian*, March 19, 2024, https://www.theguardian.com/us-news/2024/mar/19/jared-kushner-gaza-waterfront-property-israel-negev.

4. Linley Sanders, "How 5 key demographic groups voted in 2024: AP VoteCast," AP News, November 7, 2024, https://apnews.com/article/election-harris-trump-women-latinos-black-voters-0f3fbda3362f3dcfe41aa6b858f22d12.

5. Domenico Montanaro, "A Wild Year in Politics, By the Numbers," NPR, December 27, 2024, https://www.npr.org/2024/12/27/nx-s1-5222570/2024-politics-recap.

Look Ahead, Look Back *by Jason Bryan Silverstein*

1. David Oshinsky, *Worse than Slavery: Parchman Farm and the Ordeal of Jim Crow Justice* (Simon & Schuster, 1997) and Douglas A. Blackmon, *Slavery by Another Name: The Re-Enslavement of Black Americans from the Civil War to World War II* (Vintage, 2009).

2. Aspen Flynn, Adam S. Vaughan, and Michele Casper, "Differences in Geographic Patterns of Absolute and Relative Black–White Disparities in Stroke Mortality in the United States," *Preventing Chronic Disease* 19 (2022).

3. Ruhan Nagra et al., "'Waiting to Die': Toxic Emissions and Disease Near the Denka Performance Elastomer Neoprene Facility in Louisiana's Cancer Alley," *Environmental Justice* 14, no. 1 (2021): 1432.

4. Alabama Department of Public Health Center for Health Statistics, "Infant Mortality Alabama 2023," December 19, 2024.

5. Linda Villarosa, "Why America's Black Mothers and Babies Are in a Life-or-Death Crisis," *The New York Times*, April 11, 2018.

6. Martha Bebinger, "Back Bay to Nubian Square: 2 miles and a 23-year life expectancy gap," *WBUR*, May 2023.

7. Jessica Bishop-Royse et al., "Cause-Specific Mortality and Racial Differentials in Life Expectancy, Chicago 2018–2019," *Journal of Racial and Ethnic Health Disparities* 11, no. 2 (2024): 846–852.

8. Kathy Lynn Gray, "Warning: Racism Is Hazardous to Your Health in Columbus," *Columbus Monthly*, May 25, 2021.

9. Jason Silverstein, "Racial Discrimination Can Take 18 Years Off Someone's Life," *Vice*, June 12, 2018.

10. Jason Silverstein, "Genes Don't Cause Racial-Health Disparities, Society Does," *The Atlantic*, April 13, 2015.

11. Seth Holmes, *Fresh Fruit, Broken Bodies: Migrant Farmworkers in the United States* (University of California Press, 2023).
12. Eric Eyre, *Death in Mud Lick: A Coal Country Fight Against the Drug Companies That Delivered the Opioid Epidemic* (Simon & Schuster, 2020).
13. Edward Baptist, *The Half Has Never Been Told: Slavery and the Making of American Capitalism* (Hachette, 2016), and Walter Johnson, *River of Dark Dreams* (Harvard University Press, 2013).
14. Sven Beckert, *Empire of Cotton: A Global History* (Vintage, 2015).
15. Kimberly Morland et al., "Neighborhood Characteristics Associated with the Location of Food Stores and Food Service Places," *American Journal of Preventive Medicine* 22, no. 1 (2002): 23–29.

Snail's Pace: The Art of Crippling Time *by Alice Wong*

1. Ellen Samuels, "Six Ways of Looking at Crip Time," *Disability Studies Quarterly* 37, no. 3 (summer 2017).

About the Authors

Saeed Jones is the author of *Alive at the End of the World*, *How We Fight for Our Lives*, and *Prelude to Bruise*. He earned a BA at Western Kentucky University and an MFA at Rutgers University–Newark. He lives in Cambridge, Massachusetts, and is on social media @TheFerocity.

Maggie Smith is the *New York Times* bestselling author of eight books of poetry and prose, including *Good Bones*, *Dear Writer*, and *You Could Make This Place Beautiful*. Her work has appeared in *The New Yorker*, *The Paris Review*, *The Nation*, and *The Best American Poetry*. She lives in Columbus, Ohio, and is on social media @MaggieSmithPoet.

Hala Alyan is the author of the novels *Salt Houses*, winner of the Dayton Literary Peace Prize and the Arab American Book Award and a finalist for the Chautauqua Prize; and *The Arsonists' City*, a finalist for the Aspen Words Literary Prize. She is also the author of five highly acclaimed collections of poetry, including *The Twenty-Ninth Year* and *The Moon That Turns You Back*. Her work has been published by *The New Yorker*, The Academy of American Poets, *The New York Times*, *The Guardian*, and *Guernica*. She lives in Brooklyn with her family, where she works as a clinical psychologist and professor at New York University.

Eula Biss is the author of four books: *Having and Being Had*, *On Immunity*, *Notes from No Man's Land*, and *The Balloonists*. Her work has been translated into a dozen languages and has been recognized by a National Book Critics Circle Award, a Guggenheim Fellowship, a New America Fellowship, and a 21st Century Award from the Chicago Public Library. She is currently at work on a collection of essays about how private property has shaped our world.

Victoria Chang's most recent book of poems is *With My Back to the World*, published in 2024 by Farrar, Straus and Giroux in the US and Corsair/Little, Brown in the UK. It received the Forward Prize for Poetry for Best Collection and was named a finalist for the Kingsley Tufts Poetry Award and the PEN/Jean Stein Book Award. *OBIT* (Copper Canyon Press, 2020) received the Los Angeles Times Book Prize, the Anisfield-Wolf Book Award for poetry, and the PEN/Voelcker Award. It was also a finalist for the Griffin Poetry Prize and the National Book Critics Circle Award, as well as longlisted for the National Book Award. Other recent books include *The Trees Witness Everything* and her non-fiction book, *Dear Memory*. She has written several children's books as well. She has received a Guggenheim Fellowship, the Chowdhury Prize in Literature, and a National Endowment for the Arts Fellowship. She is the Bourne Chair in Poetry at Georgia Tech and Director of Poetry @ Tech.

Alexander Chee is the bestselling author of the novels *The Queen of the Night* and *Edinburgh*, and the essay collection *How to Write an Autobiographical Novel*. He is a contributing editor at the *New Republic* and an editor at large at the *Virginia Quarterly Review*. His work has appeared in *The Best American Essays* 2016 and 2019, *The New York Times Magazine*, *The New York Times Book Review*, *The New Yorker*, *T Magazine*, *Slate*, and *Vulture*, among others. He is the recipient of a 2021 Guggenheim Fellowship and a 2021 United States Artists Fellowship, and awards and fellowships from the Whiting Foundation, the NEA, and the MCCA; and residency fellowships from MacDowell, the VCCA, Civitella Ranieri, and Amtrak. He is a professor of English at Dartmouth College.

Tiana Clark is the author of the poetry collections *Scorched Earth* (Washington Square Press/Simon & Schuster, 2025) and *I Can't Talk About the Trees Without the Blood* (University of Pittsburgh Press, 2018), which won the 2017 Agnes Lynch Starrett Poetry Prize. She also wrote the chapbook *Equilibrium* (Bull City Press, 2016), selected by Afaa Michael Weaver for the 2016 Frost Place Chapbook Competition. Her writing has appeared in *The New Yorker*, *Poetry*, *The Atlantic*, *The Washington Post*, *Virginia Quarterly Review*, *The Kenyon Review*, *The Best American Poetry 2022*, and other notable publications. She was recently the Grace Hazard Conkling Writer-in-Residence at Smith College. Clark is at work on a memoir in essays, *Begging to Be Saved*, which explores Black burnout, millennial divorce, faith, art-making, and historical methods of Black survival.

Born in the Philippines in the final years of the Marcos regime, **Jill Damatac** is the author of *Dirty Kitchen*, a food memoir of growing up undocumented in America. Her writing has been featured in *The New York Times*, *Harper's Bazaar*, *British Vogue*, *The Nation*, and *The Margins*. Her film and photography work has been featured on the BBC and in *Time*; her short documentary *Blood + Ink (Dugo at Tinta)*, on Indigenous Filipino Kalinga tattooist Apo Whang-Od, was an official selection at DOC NYC and won Best Documentary at Ireland's Kerry International Film Festival. After self-deporting from the US, where she lived as an undocumented immigrant from the ages of nine to thirty-one, she earned an MA in Documentary Film from the University of the Arts London and an MSt in Creative Writing from the University of Cambridge. Damatac is now a British citizen based in the San Francisco Bay Area. She is on social media @jilldamatac.

Ashley C. Ford is the author of the *New York Times* bestseller and Oprah's Book Club pick *Somebody's Daughter*, published by Flatiron Books.

Ford has written or guest-edited for *The New York Times*, *The Guardian*, *ELLE*, *BuzzFeed*, *Slate*, *Teen Vogue*, *New York* magazine, and more. She is the current host of Ben & Jerry's *Into the Mix* podcast.

She's taught creative nonfiction at The New School in Manhattan and Aspen Summer Words, and served as Ball State University's Writer-in-Residence.

Ford lives in Indianapolis, Indiana, with her husband, poet

and fiction writer Kelly Stacy, and their chocolate lab, Astro Renegade Ford-Stacy.

Joy Harjo is the author of ten books of poetry, most recently *Weaving Sundown in a Scarlet Light*, several plays, several prose collections and children's books, and two memoirs, *Crazy Brave* and *Poet Warrior*; she has also produced seven award-winning music albums and edited several anthologies, including *When the Light of the World Was Subdued, Our Songs Came Through: A Norton Anthology of Native Nations Poetry*. Her many honors include the Poetry Society of America's 2024 Frost Medal, Yale's 2023 Bollingen Prize for American Poetry, and a 2022 National Humanities Medal. She served as a chancellor of the Academy of American Poets and a founding chair of the Native Arts + Cultures Foundation, and she is the inaugural Artist-in-Residence for Tulsa's Bob Dylan Center. A member of the Muscogee Nation, Harjo served three terms as the twenty-third poet laureate of the United States. She lives on the Muscogee Nation reservation in Oklahoma.

Aubrey Hirsch is the author of *Graphic Rage: Comics on Gender, Justice, and Life as a Woman in America*. Her comics, essays, and stories have appeared in *The New York Times*, *The Washington Post*, *Vox*, *The Nib*, *Time*, and elsewhere. She is the recipient of a National Endowment for the Arts Fellowship in literature and an Individual Award from the Sustainable Arts Foundation.

Mira Jacob is a novelist, memoirist, illustrator, and cultural critic. Her graphic memoir *Good Talk: A Memoir in Conversations* was shortlisted for the National Book Critics Circle Award, longlisted for the PEN Open Book Award, and named a *New York Times* Notable Book. Her novel *The Sleepwalker's Guide to Dancing* was a Barnes & Noble Discover Great New Writers pick and named one of the best books of the year by *Kirkus Reviews*, *The Boston Globe*, and Goodreads. She is a professor at The New School and a founding faculty member of the MFA in writing at Randolph College.

Marlon James was born in Jamaica in 1970. His most recent novel, *Moon Witch, Spider King*, is the second novel in his Dark Star fantasy trilogy. *Black Leopard, Red Wolf*, the first novel in the Dark Star trilogy, was a finalist for the 2019 National Book Award. His novel *A Brief History of Seven Killings* was the winner of the 2015 Man Booker Prize. He is also the author of the novels *John Crow's Devil* and *The Book of Night Women*, which won the Dayton Literary Peace Prize.

Kay Jones is an editor and writer living in the Pacific Northwest with her son, partner, and dog. You can find her on most social media as @KayJonesPNW.

Aruni Kashyap writes in English and Assamese and is an associate professor of English at the University of Georgia. He is the author of *The Way You Want to Be Loved*, *The House with a Thousand Stories*, and the forthcoming *How to Date a Fanatic*. Along with editing the story collection *How to Tell the Story of an Insurgency*, he is the translator of four novels from Assamese to English. A 2024 Carl and Lily Pforzheimer Foundation Fellow at Radcliffe Institute for Advanced Study at Harvard University, he is also the recipient of a National Endowment for the Arts Fellowship, the Faculty Research Grants in the Humanities and Arts program, the Arts Lab Faculty Fellowship, and the Charles Wallace India Trust Scholarship for Creative Writing at the University of Edinburgh. His poetry collection, *There Is No Good Time for Bad News*, was nominated for the fifty-eighth Georgia Author of the Year Awards 2022, and was a finalist for the Marsh Hawk Press Poetry Prize and the Four Way Books Levis Prize in Poetry.

Kiese Laymon is a Black southern writer from Jackson, Mississippi. The author of several books, including *Heavy: An American Memoir*, he is the Moody Professor of Creative Writing and English at Rice University.

Ada Limón is the author of seven books of poetry, including *Startlement: New & Selected Poems*; *The Hurting Kind*, which was a finalist for the Griffin Poetry Prize; *The Carrying*, which won the National Books Critics Circle Award and was a finalist for the PEN/Jean Stein Book Award; and *Bright Dead Things*, which was named a finalist for the National Book Award, the National Book Critics Circle Award, and the Kingsley Tufts Award. Limón is the recipient of a MacArthur Fellowship and a Guggenheim Fellowship and was named a 2024 *Time* Woman of the Year. She is the author of two picture books, *In Praise of Mystery* and *And, Too, the Fox*, as well as the editor of the anthology *You Are Here: Poetry in the Natural World*. She served as the twenty-fourth poet laureate of the United States.

Randall Mann is the author of six poetry collections, most recently *Deal: New and Selected Poems* (Copper Canyon Press, 2023). He works in biotech, teaches at the Bennington College Writing Seminars, and lives in San Francisco.

Abi Maxwell is the author of two novels and, most recently, the memoir *One Day I'll Grow Up and Be a Beautiful Woman*. She is a graduate of the writing program at the University of Montana, a former librarian, and a dedicated advocate for the rights of transgender youth. She spent the last seven years focused on creating safe schools and fighting against anti-trans legislation in her home state of New Hampshire. However, in July 2024, after anti-trans legislation began to be signed into law, her family relocated to California, where she continues to write fiction and nonfiction as well as advocate for LGBTQ+ youth.

Koritha Mitchell is a literary historian and cultural critic. She is the feminist scholar who coined the term *know-your-place aggression* to emphasize that marginalized groups are attacked for succeeding, not because they have done something wrong. Mitchell is author of *Living with Lynching* and *From Slave Cabins to the White House.* She is also editor of the first book-length autobiography by a formerly enslaved African American woman, Harriet Jacobs's *Incidents in the Life of a Slave Girl* (1861). Her public commentary has appeared in outlets such as *Time, Black Perspectives, The Washington Post,* the *Los Angeles Review of Books,* MSNBC, CNN, and *Good Morning America.* In 2023, she was recognized as a champion of women in the public sphere with a Progressive Women's Voices IMPACT Award from the Women's Media Center. After eighteen years at Ohio State University, Mitchell now teaches at Boston University. Online, she's @ProfKori and at korithamitchell.com.

Imani Perry is the Henry A. Morss, Jr. and Elisabeth W. Morss Professor of Studies of Women, Gender and Sexuality and of African and African American Studies at Harvard University, and the Carol K. Pforzheimer Professor at Harvard Radcliffe Institute. Perry is the author of nine books, including the *New York Times* bestseller *South to America: A Journey Below the Mason-Dixon to Understand the Soul of a Nation,* which received the 2022 National Book Award for Nonfiction. Her most recent book is *Black in Blues: How a Color Tells the Story of My People.* Perry has written for numerous publications, including *The New*

York Times, *The Atlantic*, *Oxford American*, *Harper's*, and *Harper's Bazaar*. She is a 2023 recipient of a MacArthur Genius Fellowship. Perry has also received fellowships from the Guggenheim Foundation and the Pew Center.

Sam Sax is the author of the novel *Yr Dead* (longlisted for the National Book Award) and the poetry collections *Pig* (named a best book of 2023 by *Vulture* and *Electric Lit*), *Bury It* (winner of the James Laughlin Award), and *Madness* (winner of the National Poetry Series). They live in Oakland, California, and lecture in the Interdisciplinary Arts program at Stanford University.

Jason Bryan Silverstein is an anthropologist and writer-in-residence in the Department of Global Health and Social Medicine at Harvard Medical School, where he cofounded the Media, Medicine, and Health Program. His reporting and essays on racism, health, and human rights have appeared in *Vice*, *GQ*, *The Atlantic*, and elsewhere. He lives in Cambridge, Massachusetts, with his daughter, Mallory.

Danez Smith is the author of four collections, including *Don't Call Us Dead*; *Homie*; and most recently *Bluff*. They are also the curator of *Blues in Stereo: The Early Works of Langston Hughes*. For their work, Smith won the Forward Prize for Best Collection, the

Minnesota Book Award, and the Lambda Literary Award and has been a finalist for the NAACP Image Award, the National Book Critics Circle Award, and the National Book Award. Smith lives in the Twin Cities with their people.

Patricia Smith is the author of nine books of poetry, including *The Intentions of Thunder: New and Selected Poems*; *Unshuttered*; *Incendiary Art*, winner of the Kingsley Tufts Poetry Award, the Los Angeles Times Book Prize, the NAACP Image Award, and a finalist for the Pulitzer Prize; *Shoulda Been Jimi Savannah*, winner of the Lenore Marshall Poetry Prize from the Academy of American Poets; and *Blood Dazzler*, a National Book Award finalist. Her work has been published widely, including in *The Best American Poetry* and *The Best American Essays* anthologies; her short story "When They Are Done with Us" won the Robert L. Fish Memorial Award from the Mystery Writers of America and was featured in *The Best American Mystery Stories.*

Smith is a 2024 inductee into the Chicago Literary Hall of Fame, as well as a member of the American Academy of Arts and Sciences; a chancellor in the Academy of American Poets; a Guggenheim Fellow; a National Endowment for the Arts grant recipient; a finalist for the Neustadt International Prize for Literature; a former fellow at Civitella Ranieri, Yaddo, and MacDowell; and a four-time individual champion of the National Poetry Slam, the most successful poet in the competition's history.

She is a professor at the Lewis Center for the Arts at Princeton University, as well as a former distinguished professor for the City University of New York. Currently, she is at work on her first novel and a collection of short stories.

Chase Strangio is a lawyer at the American Civil Liberties Union (ACLU), where he litigates cases on behalf of LGBTQ people. He has been involved in some of the most pivotal queer and trans civil rights cases of the past decade, including *Obergefell v. Hodges*, *Bostock v. Clayton County*, and *United States v. Skrmetti*. Strangio lives in New York City with his twelve-year-old child and his four-year-old cat.

Alice Wong (she/her) is a disabled activist, writer, editor, and community organizer. She is the founder of the Disability Visibility Project, an online community dedicated to creating, sharing, and amplifying disability media and culture. Wong is the editor of *Disability Visibility: First-Person Stories from the Twenty-First Century*, an anthology of essays by disabled people, and *Disability Visibility: 17 First-Person Stories for Today*, an adapted version for young adults. Her debut memoir, *Year of the Tiger: An Activist's Life*, was published in 2022. Her latest anthology, *Disability Intimacy: Essays on Love, Care, and Desire*, is available now. In 2024, Wong was named a MacArthur Fellow.